Octu

SELF-TRAINING IN PRAYER

LONDON AGENTS:—

SIMPKIN, MARSHALL & CO. LTD.

SELF-TRAINING IN PRAYER

A. H. McNEILE, D.D.,

Fellow and Dean of Sidney Sussex College, Cambridge

"Despise not thy prayer, for He to whom thou prayest despiseth it not."
S. BERNARD.

CAMBRIDGE
W. HEFFER & SONS LTD
1918

FIRST PRINTED - - - · MARCH, 1916

SECOND IMPRESSION - - - JULY, 1916
(with slight additions)

THIRD IMPRESSION - - AUGUST, 1916

FOURTH IMPRESSION - - JANUARY, 1917

FIFTH IMPRESSION - - - MAY, 1917

SIXTH IMPRESSION - - JUNE, 1918
(making 19,000 copies.)

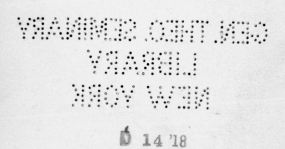

CONTENTS.

PREFACE.

THE following pages have arisen out of four lectures delivered in the church of S. Botolph, Cambridge, in the Lent term of this year.

In the turmoil of our surface life there is a multitude of men and women who would give anything to be able to look through it and see God. Many of them pray, but seldom feel that they are doing something *real*. They cannot launch out into the deep, and let down their nets for a draught from the ocean of Reality. Prayer is to them a religious duty rather than a religious experience.

It is to such that these suggestions are offered. For it is the deepening consciousness of the reality of prayer that alone will make Christian England to become Christian after the war. Without it, all the schemes of all the brains in the Empire will not bring about what we long for—that when there is peace on earth there shall also be glory to God in the highest.

A. H. M^cNEILE.

Cambridge, Quinquagesima, 1916.

I. REALITY IN PRAYER.

PRAYER may be looked at from different points of view, as either a problem, a phenomenon, or a profession. As a philosophical problem it involves other problems, such as those connected with the so-called ' laws of Nature ' and miracle, divine foreknowledge and determination, and man's will and power of voluntary action. As an historical phenomenon it is a fascinating study ; it may be traced from the most primitive of savage incantations till it reaches its highest development in the life of Christian saints. As problem or as phenomenon alone, it is of purely academic interest ; but whatever may be the best word to use as a counterpart to ' academic,' that word must be applied to prayer as a profession. It is a subject that is intensely alive to those who believe in it and practise it. And this book is written for no one else. There is only one object that I would ask you to set before you in reading these pages, and that is to study prayer in such a way as to gain a deeper and more vivid understanding of its aliveness. To study prayer is not simply to study a book about it, but to make the suggestions which the book contains, if they are of any value, a guide in a long, diligent course of self-training. A beginner should set himself to practise them, as he would work through the exercises in a grammar. In a sermon on the subject it would be natural for a preacher to try and rouse his audience to pray *more*. Probably none of us prays enough. But it is far more important to learn how to pray *better*. At best 'we know not what we should pray for as we ought'; the Holy Spirit must do that for us 'with unutterable groanings,' because at present we know only in part, and pray as well as prophesy in part. But even in this partial power that we possess there are many different degrees. Some Christians are advanced experts, and others the most elementary beginners. It is a common experience, however, that the advanced expert is not always the most suitable person to teach the elements of a subject, and that is why I can venture to offer these suggestions.

We are all longing that England may become a better England after the war, and numberless ideas are afloat as to how to make it so. We know that many thousands of men and women are not Christians at all, and need to be converted. But I am sure—and I say it as deliberately and earnestly as I can—that the great and crying need is that those who are Christians should learn to pray better. So many do not think of it as the profession of their lives, for which they need training, practice, experience, just as truly as a doctor, or nurse, or school teacher. If Christianity is to spread, it must be spread by Christians, and the one and only effective means of doing so is not argument but holiness, which includes prayer.

Let us begin with our Lord's words in S. Matt. vi. 7 : 'When ye pray, use not idle words'—our English translation, 'use not vain repetitions,' does not really represent the force of the Greek—'use not idle words as the heathen do, for they think that they shall be heard for their much speaking.' And don't some English Christians think the same ? or at any rate act as if they thought so ? They use many books of devotion, they attend many services, they say many prayers ; but all the time they know, at the bottom of their hearts, that a great deal of it is idle words. Carry your mind back to last Sunday, or the last time you were present at a Church service, and ask yourself—How much of that service was, in my case, real prayer, and not merely listening, or possibly wool-gathering, while prayers were being read ? S. Augustine has a characteristic comment on our Lord's words. He says that our prayers ought to contain not *multa locutio*, but *multa precatio*—' not much speaking, but much prayer.' Our great difficulty is not to say a great many prayers, but to make our prayers alive, and vivid, and real.

Not long ago I read an article in a Church paper entitled ' What's wrong with the laity ? ' I have very little doubt as to the answer. The mass of English people are losing their hold on religion, or perhaps I should say religion is losing its hold on them, because for some centuries past its *reality* has been gradually fading from their lives. God is not real to them, nor Christ, nor the Holy Spirit ; this world is real to them, but not the other. And prayer, instead of being the centre and mainspring of their lives, has become a mere appendage, a nice little habit tacked on to them as children with their pinafores, and given up when they put away childish things. Nothing will make England Christian till England has learnt to pray. And in the same Church paper, soon afterwards, someone retorted with the question : ' What's wrong with the clergy ? ' And I believe the true answer is precisely the same. A terribly large percentage of the clergy needs to be converted. They are obliged, by their profession, to say many prayers ; but the best men among them would confess that they very often use idle words, because their prayers are lacking in reality. The first step in our self-training is to recognise our need.

At this point the reader who wants to make full use of these pages is advised to kneel down and think slowly and quietly about himself, to find out how great his need really is. In his daily life—his work, recreation, walks, meals, conversations—how small a place is occupied by God ! How seldom he remembers Him, or does the small daily actions for His sake, with the conscious wish to give Him pleasure because he loves Him !

II. NATURE.

NOW dwell on the word Reality. Look at
a rose in summer, arrayed as Solomon in
all his glory was not arrayed, and try to think
what it *really is*. Ask the botanist and the
biologist to help you, and they will describe,
probably with many Latin words, its genus
and family, all its parts, its growth and
its habits. But that won't tell you what
a rose really is. You call in a mathematician, and by means of geometry and
trigonometry he might be able to tell you all
about its curves and planes ; its form and shape
could, theoretically at any rate, be mapped out
in diagrams. But that wouldn't express the
real rose in its sensuous and compelling love-
liness. Or, once more, the chemist could tell
you the part played by sun and rain, air and
soil ; he might explain the causes of colour and

scent. But the real rose would be as far off as ever. Something affects you which is deeper and more mysterious than all this, something intangible, invisible, but which appeals to you as infinitely more real than anything which your senses can grasp. And we call it *Life*. Your eye passes to another rose, to a lily, to a hundred other revelations of beauty. And as you feast yourself upon them, you know that it is one and the same Life that makes them all what they are. You cut a shoot off the rose-bush and plant it, and it makes roots for itself, and yields you another rose. It is the same Life, expressing itself by means of sun and air and soil, shape and colour and scent.

Now yield yourself to that thought ; deliver yourself up to the unspeakable Reality which is the source of your garden's beauty. And then let yourself wander on through all the vast tracts of the earth, and then through all the dizzy tracts of the universe ; and try to feel that what is true of the rose must be true of all that is. Goethe expressed the truth in a sentence when he said, ' Everything transitory is parable ' ; in other words, everything material is only a temporary outward and visible instrument by which Life—Reality—expresses itself.

I think it is probably true to say that the great majority of people have done very little indeed towards getting into touch with Reality in this way. They enjoy what meets their senses, but they don't penetrate to its Source. Those who do it most successfully are the true artists, the painters and poets and musicians and all the people whom we call geniuses. But it is possible for everyone to do it to some extent, if they set to work to train their faculties to that end. An artist of any kind is born, not made; but many a born artist has remained undiscovered, even by himself, because his natural faculties have not been given a proper chance of doing their work. I am not, however, asking anyone to try to become an artist, but to try to gain a little more of the wealth of interest and beauty that is added to life when he can feel, or perceive, or realise, the divine Reality behind and within everything in the universe.

This Life, or Reality, which is the only real thing in Nature, is sometimes described as 'supernatural'; but the word is apt to be misleading, because to so many minds it suggests something unreal. We might coin the word 'intranatural,' 'within the natural'; but we must get rid of all notion of space or locality. Music is not locally in a violin when it is expressed by means of a violin. And the divine Reality is not locally in Nature, but expresses itself by means of Nature.

But next let us ask—If it is there, why don't we all realise it naturally? Well, suppose we could imagine a person born, and brought up, and living unceasingly, in a certain light, or with a certain sound always in his ears, or a certain scent always in his nostrils. It would be very difficult for him to realise the fact of such a light, or sound, or scent. He could do it only by a special concentration of thought upon it. Having been told that it existed, he would have to bring himself into such a condition that he could disregard everything else that met his senses, and strive with his whole being to realise that one thing which always surrounded him. He could do it gradually, if he went the right way to work. This thought of concentration is very important, and will come before us again.

To realise the divine Reality in Nature to ever so small an extent, to wonder at it, and enjoy it, and to be lifted out of ourselves by it, is what is called Natural Religion, or the Religion of Nature. And some of the artistic geniuses who do it well and easily are so engrossed and enraptured that they feel as though they were satisfied by it, and so they never get any further.

They are so entirely enthralled by the cult of Beauty that they have no thought or conception of anything better. And if to this Reality, which they reach by means of Nature, they give the name God, and find Him in no other way, they are what we call Pantheists. The truth contained in Pantheism is gloriously true so far as it goes ; but by itself it is only a half truth, and therefore false. But since truth is in it, it ought not to be neglected by the Christian. In our self-training in prayer it is a real help to practise that inner concentration by which we can pass through Nature, which is seen and temporal and therefore symbolic and unreal, to that which is unseen and eternal and therefore the only Reality. That is the nearest approach to prayer that the Pantheist can make ; and many of them do make it to a wonderful extent, which puts many Christians to shame. It is, in fact, an urgent call to us for self-scrutiny. It is worth while to pause here before passing to the next chapter, and to think whether, in this respect, you have not been shutting the eyes of your soul to Reality,—revelling, perhaps, in the sense-enjoyment of Nature, but making very little effort to get, by means of it, into touch with the Divine. Recognise your need, and then begin at once to practise, and to train

yourself at every opportunity to realise that
every beautiful object in Nature is an instrument
by which God is expressing Himself. We know
it theoretically ; sometimes we thank Him for
it ; but to very few is it real.

NOTE.—A correspondent writes, "What are we to say
about ugly things ?" I think that we may reply by
adapting S. Paul's words in Romans xiv. 14: "There
is nothing ugly of itself ; but to him that esteemeth
any thing to be ugly, to him it is ugly." Ugliness is
my description of the unpleasant effect produced upon
me by the physical appearance of a thing. The effect
is akin to pain. Heat, light, sound, taste, may each be
pleasant to a certain degree of intensity, but if the
intensity increases they become painful. And they may
be pleasant for one person to a much greater degree
of intensity than for another. It is impossible to say
that they are instruments of God's Self-expression only
as long as they are pleasant, and not when they become
unpleasant. The problem of ugliness, as of pain, is as
difficult for our limited intelligence as the problem of
man's will, which can, and does, set itself in opposition
to God's will. But it is not to be solved by a dualism
which excludes from His all-reaching activity things
which do not cause us physical sensations of pleasure.

III. PERSONS.

WHEN we pass from the half truth in Pantheism to the whole truth in Christianity, our thoughts must move in the same direction, but on a higher plane. The Christian has learnt that the supreme, the only, Reality—that which expresses itself impersonally in Nature—is *personal*. We can speak of He, not of It. Personality has been defined as 'the capacity for fellowship,' that is the capacity for self-communication to persons, communion, mutual response, mutual indwelling, real union, with persons. So that I am able to say—God is in me; God is in you. But remember, all idea of locality must be avoided. It is not a little bit of God inside me, and a little bit of God inside you, any more than we can say that there is a little bit of music inside one violin and a little bit of music inside another violin. It is God, the one infinite Reality, who reveals Himself as physical life in all Nature, and as

personal character in man. The two-fold
truth is stated in the Prologue of the Fourth
Gospel : ' All things were made by Him, and
without Him was not anything made that was
made ; in Him was Life.' Thus far the evange
list describes Reality in Nature. But then
comes the leap to the higher plane : ' The Life
was the Light of men.' That is what makes all
mankind one. As individuals, men are only
instruments, symbols, 'parables,' to use Goethe's
word, of the Infinite and the Eternal. But as
personal, mankind is one communion and
fellowship. And the more we can annul our
individual Self, the more free we are to realise
our oneness with the Whole. He that loseth
his Self shall find it.

But the Whole, in its ideal and complete perfection, proceeding eternally from God, existing
eternally as the Object of God's love and
thought, and expressed in time in the Person of
Jesus Christ, is the Second Person of the Holy
Trinity. And dwelling in us, manifesting,
expressing Himself by means of us, is His
Spirit, the Third Person of the Holy Trinity.
S. Paul had a clear grasp of the two-fold truth.
He describes the purpose for which God converted him in the words ' It pleased God . . .
to reveal His Son in me ' (Gal. i. 15) ; God did

not convert Saul merely for his own sake, but that he might become an instrument by which the divine personal Reality should express Himself. And exactly parallel with that is his description of the use which God makes of all Christians : ' There are diversities of workings, but the same God who worketh all in all. But to each one is given the manifestation of the Spirit for the (general) advantage ' (I. Cor. xii. 6, 7). The Holy Spirit manifests, expresses Himself in all Christians as instruments, or, as S. Paul puts it later in the chapter, in all the several members of the one Body of Christ.

IV. THE ESSENCE OF PRAYER.

THE thought of divine Reality expressing Himself personally by means of persons carries us to the heart of our subject. What exactly is Prayer ? I hope that all that has been said so far will have helped to lead us to a definition. Prayer is not petition, or intercession, or praise, or thanksgiving, or meditation, or contemplation. These are, so to speak, the bookwork of the subject ; they are the grammar and vocabulary of the celestial language. And self-training requires that they shall be worked at with steady, plodding, perseverance, in order that we may arrive at its very spirit and meaning. They are methods, which we shall study later ; roads by which we can travel towards our goal. But the goal itself, the inner essence of Prayer is one and the same. It is *by a deliberate act of our whole being to make real to ourselves the divine Reality*. That which is divinely personal in us reaches after the personal God who wants to reveal Himself through us. It is the act of realising Christ in us and in all men, of arriving at a consciousness of His Spirit in us and in all men. A Christian at prayer is like a living violin striving to realise, to immerse itself consciously in, the musician's soul of which it is an instrument. That which the artist does by the consideration of material nature, the Christian does, on a higher plane, by prayer. 'The Life was the Light of men.' Light is one of the greatest of Biblical metaphors for the divine, personal Reality revealing Himself in man, and found perfectly in Christ. And the aim of prayer is to gain a real inner perception of the Light.

But to how many Christians do words like these convey any vivid meaning ? A sign of the extent to which English Christians fail in the matter of prayer is the meaning which they attach to the word 'faith.' We read 'Blessed are they that have not seen, and yet have believed'; and S. Paul says 'We walk by faith, not by sight.' Such sayings mean that we must not wait to accept spiritual truths until we are convinced of them by proofs supplied through our bodily senses, or arrived at intellectually by logical deduction. But many people are apt to make 'faith' equivalent to what is called 'blind faith,' a nominal acceptance of untried truths simply on the testimony of others—the testimony of the Bible, or of the experience of other Christians.

There is, indeed, another misuse of the word 'faith,' which has to do with answers to prayer. Some people make it mean a feeling of certainty that God will give something that He is asked for, which, if they could only contrive to feel it, would be an infallible magic in procuring whatever they happen to want. And when God doesn't give just what they happen to want, because it would not help forward His plans for them and for mankind, they conclude mournfully that the reason must have been their want of faith.

Both of these are caricatures of real faith. Faith is that which enables us to say 'We speak that we do know, and testify that we have seen.' The Queen of Sheba heard a report in her own land of Solomon's wealth and wisdom ; and she was willing to accept the information as trustworthy. But when she came—that was the real act of faith—and saw it with her own eyes, she said ' Behold the half was not told me.

> 'But what to those who find? Ah! this
>   Nor tongue nor pen can shew ;
> The love of Jesus, what it is
>   None but His loved ones know.

It is quite right to begin by taking the fact of
Christ for granted on the report of others ; but
it is something unspeakably different when we
reach actual personal experience. That is the
crying need of to-day. The faith in Christ of
so very many Christians is still nominal, and
theoretical, and conventional. ' The Incarnate, Crucified, and Risen Christ is the only
Reality—our salvation and strength and glory
and joy ? Yes, oh yes, so I've been told ; and I
quite believe it. That is why I say my prayers
and go to Church.' But it isn't *real* to them.
We want to be able to say, as the Samaritans
said to the woman, ' Now we believe, not
because of thy speaking, for we have heard for
ourselves.' ' Oh come hither and hearken, all
ye that fear God, and I will tell you what He
hath done for my soul ! ' That is the result of
' faith.' Faith is the action of the whole being
which drives a man to make experiment, to gain
living experience, of the divine Reality ; and
Prayer *is* the experiment and the experience.

V. PENITENCE AND HUMILITY.

WE must next turn to a thought of quite immeasurable importance. If the divine Reality, which wants to express itself, is personal, and possesses character, it can be realised in actual experience only by persons possessed of character akin to it. In other words, that which destroys our power of experiencing Reality, and hinders us from reaching after union with it, is Sin. The pure in heart shall see God. Perfect sinlessness alone can be in complete oneness with infinite perfection. It is only by being united with Christ's sinlessness, by being 'accepted in the Beloved,' that we can begin to catch the faintest spiritual glimpse of the personal Reality. But to be accepted in the Beloved means to be forgiven by God. And therefore at every stage in our self-training no step in advance is conceivable without *Penitence*. We are always surrounded by the limitless ocean of God's love, but like the shellfish we can shut it out. When penitence opens the shell, the love of God immediately, 'automatically,' floods our heart, and we are forgiven,

But as long as we have one sin knowingly un-repented of, one sin from which we don't really want to be free, any approach to Reality is absolutely barred. Sin is the assertion of our individual Self, the separation of our individual Self from the infinite Person. Sin is the act of moving away from God ; and since prayer is the act of moving into union with Him, sin and prayer are a contradiction in terms.

And from Penitence *Humility* is born. It sounds hard, but it must be said : You cannot pray, you cannot get into touch with divine Reality, except in proportion to your humility ; your selflessness ; your readiness, for example, to take a rebuke or a slight without resentment, to give a real meaning to S. Paul's words ' in honour preferring one another,' to esteem others better than yourself. You can pray only in proportion as you ' have this mind in you which was also in Christ Jesus, who . . . emptied Himself . . . humbled Himself, becoming obedient even to (the climax of) death, yea the death of the Cross.' ' Becoming obedient.' That is to most of us a matter of desperate difficulty. Sheer humble obedience to God's will, in whatever form, or by whatever means, it may make itself known to us, whether through the guidance of circumstances, or the call of conscience, or—what is often harder to accept—through other people.

And beside the difficulty of obedience there is the difficulty of readiness to be in the background, to be unnoticed, and passed over, to take trouble and to receive in return little or no praise or acknowledgment or thanks. Everyone has felt the thousand pin-pricks of life, which hurt so horribly while we are diseased with Self-love. They usurp our whole attention, they keep our thought and memory engrossed. While we are feeling resentment, pride, touchiness, temper, and such like, we cannot feel God. While we are in the grip of Self we cannot be free to fling out our arms in a yearning grasp of the Infinite and the Eternal.

So we begin to see why it is that the great masters of the spiritual life who have taught the world how to pray, one and all without exception, began and carried on their self-training with penitence, self-mortification, struggles against sin, humility, selflessness. Every branch in the True Vine that beareth fruit, even to the extent of the first new-born desire to feel after Him and find Him, the Father purgeth that it may bring forth more fruit. And if He does it by sorrow, anxiety, or pain, it is for the same all-loving purpose.

However far you advance, however close the union with God to which you attain, the purging must still go on, that you may bear more and more fruit, and learn obedience by the things that you suffer.

And isn't that exactly the meaning of Baptism ? Union with the Divine Life by means of a death unto sin. The struggle of the Christian towards God is simply the continuation, the making real and actual, of the New Birth in Baptism.

Before passing on to the next chapter I would ask you to undergo again a long quiet self-scrutiny, to determine, as fully and ruthlessly as you can, the ways—perhaps the many ways—in which Self asserts its claims in your life ; the ways in which you find obedience and humility peculiarly difficult. And then offer a prayer of penitence.

The first part of our subject is now completed. I hope that the reader will not be surprised that up to this point practically nothing has been said about prayer as it is usually understood. What I am trying to do is precisely to get away from the ordinary, conventional ideas about prayer, and to carry our minds to the point of view of those who knew more about it by experience than most of us have attained to—

people like S. Augustine, S. Bernard, S. Teresa, Brother Laurence, and many others ; and behind them the apostles and prophets on whom the Church is built ; and behind them Jesus Christ Himself the head Corner-Stone. All these knew by vivid, compelling, personal experience that prayer is not a mere telephoning to God to ask Him to do things, but a developing life, an expanding, deepening, heightening, intensifying, of the whole being, by allowing it to be drawn in the embrace of God nearer and nearer to Himself.

VI. INFLUENCE.

THE second part of our subject will still not be prayer as ordinarily understood. Nevertheless it brings before us an aspect of our self-training whose importance cannot be exaggerated. In chapter iii. it was said that because the divine Reality makes mankind the instrument of His personal Self-expression, the medium through which He reveals Himself— in other words because ' the Life was the Light of men '—*all mankind is one*. If you tell some people that, they will shrug their shoulders and say ' No doubt there is a sense in which it is theoretically true ; but practically it is nonsense ; mankind is many and not one.' To speak of the solidarity of man is a playing with words, a fanciful absurdity, to those whose thoughts are bound to the transitory, material, surface things of life. But for self-training in prayer it is all-important to try and gain a vivid grasp of it as a real truth. The tendency of the modern Western mind is towards Individualism, but it is a tendency which leads away from prayer. That is one of the reasons why true prayer—the real thing—has been fading away from so many lives.

When we approach the conception of the one-ness of mankind, we must try to lift it out of vagueness, and to change it from an abstraction or a poetical figure of speech into a clear cut and appealing fact. And I think that the best way to do that is to study what we call *Influence*. It will show us what we want to see in—one might almost say—an outward and visible form. Consider the word itself. Who-ever was responsible for coining it went a long way towards explaining the idea. ' Influence ' is derived from the same word as ' Influx,' a ' pouring or flowing in.' Any word involving the thought of motion in space, if it is employed to describe that which is non-material, must be recognised as metaphorical. But this is, at least, an extremely good metaphor. Influence is the pouring in of personality into personality ; it is the interpenetration of souls. An officer is in a trench with his men, and the order comes to make a charge. He leads the way with the courage of a true man, shouts a rousing word of encouragement, and pours courage into the whole of his company. But think what that means. Courage is not an unreal abstraction, but, on the other hand, it is not a thing in itself with an existence separate from the officer. It is *his* courage which he pours into them, an ingredient of the person flowing into other persons. May we not say that Influence, looked at in this way, becomes a clear cut and appealing fact ? Courage does not *leave* the officer. On the contrary his courage grows, because in rousing his men to courage, he in turn receives theirs poured into him. It is a mutual influx of personalities. But I think we may go further, and say that all the soldiers who are fighting bravely in Europe and Asia and Africa, whether of the allies or of the enemy, are severally items in one complex system of Influence. The mutual give-and-take of courage extends over three continents. And more than that, it extends to thousands who are not fighting ; the courage of the wounded, the courage of those who are maimed for life, the courage of prisoners of war, and the courage of multitudes of men and women who are bravely bearing sorrow, anxiety, and strain. It is one communion and fellowship of courageous souls, every one of whom is poured into all the others.

But that is only one minute specimen of Influence. When one person receives it from another, whether in the form of courage or of any other ingredient of the soul, it can flow on from him into others without diminishing in the process, and with no limits of possibility. All mankind, past and present, form one communion and fellowship, one inconceivably complex system of interpenetration. If you think it out, it is a frightening thought—the immeasurable responsibility of every soul in its effects upon the whole of mankind. It is parallel with what we are told is the case in the physical universe. In a paper entitled *The Modern Conception of the Universe** Dr. G. F. C. Searle writes : ' The effects of a single act of free-will extend through the whole of space, and will last as long as the present order continues. Thus the voluntary motion of a man's hand not only affects the motion of the earth by a calculable amount, but also the motions of the sun and of the remotest stars, and the motions of all these bodies will differ for the rest of time from the motions they would have had if the man had not moved his hand.'

And if it is a frightening thought, it is also extraordinarily humbling when it is once clearly grasped. The words I and Me begin to be a little less clear cut and obtrusive. We begin to see that it is not only proud but also

---

* Pan-Anglican Papers, S.P.C.K., 1908.

very silly to lay so much stress on our individual Self, when we realise that the soul of each of us is conditioned, to so enormous an extent, by the interplay of all souls.

Influence, then, is an almost visible exhibition of the oneness of mankind. If you dwell on it, and allow yourself quietly to be steeped in the notion of the interpenetration of personalities, you can come almost to see it. On certain occasions, with certain groups or bodies of people collected together, it is peculiarly vivid. Sometimes when you and another person are alone together, you can affect each other intensely ; something seems to pass and re-pass between you so real that you feel as though you can, so to speak, cut it with a knife. But apart from these special instances, it is possible to gain a real grasp of the truth as a whole. And we must remember that it is not only the influence of which we are conscious that counts, but also that far greater mass of which we are unconscious, that is poured out by, and stored up in, what is popularly called our sub-consciousness, and shows itself perhaps long afterwards in word or deed or thought or habit. It all goes to shape character.

This wonderful system of mutuality between souls is an instance of something which it is very hard to grasp because we always live in it. But the reader is strongly advised, if he wishes to excel in prayer, to make a frequent and diligent practice of concentrating himself upon it, until it emerges and takes shape as one of the most compelling objects of his thought.

VII. CHARACTER.

LET us go further, and see what follows from this. If all souls interpenetrate, mankind is not merely a jumble of different characters, like a box-full of differently coloured marbles. Mankind, as one real whole, possesses one real character, the net result, at any given moment, of the whole process of its spiritual life. Every thought, word, and deed of every individual either lifts up or drags down, either improves or spoils, the net character of the whole, because every thought, word, and deed affects his own character, and therefore his influence. If one member suffer—spiritually—all the members suffer with it.

To grasp this truly and thoroughly is to arrive at a motive for holiness, and therefore a motive for prayer, which is free from all taint of Self. ' For their sake I sanctify myself '— in order to lift up the net character of mankind. But when we speak of lifting up, or dragging down, the character of mankind, we mean drawing it nearer to, or further from, the

Character of God. That is the character that He wants to reveal and express in mankind as His instrument. It is the character of mankind as He thinks and plans it, and works and longs for it. In other words it is the Character of the Incarnate, Crucified, and Risen Christ, Eternal, Human, Universal, the perfect expression of God, offering His life and power and perfection to every soul who wants to lift up the character of men.

VIII. PRIESTHOOD.

ALL that has been said in the foregoing pages leads to the thought of Priesthood, which is quite fundamental in Christianity, and without which prayer is well nigh emptied of all meaning.

An ambassador at a foreign court communicates the will of his government. In that act his individual self is by the nature of the case blotted out and non-existent. His nation as a single whole expresses itself by means of him ; he is a point at which the whole of one nation can come into contact with the whole of another nation.

And every human being is similarly representative of the whole of mankind. But to grasp the oneness of mankind, and the oneness of its character, and our representative relation to it, to concentrate ourselves upon it, to ponder it, and at last to feel it, is to feel the shame of the sin of the world—not only the shame of *my* sin, because it spoils *my* character, but the shame of all men's sin, because it wrongs the Father of

love, who wants to express Himself perfectly in
man. The closer that we approach to union
with Reality, the more we shall, as a mediæval
writer puts it, ' feel sin as a lump '—feel all sin
as one vast mass of crushing defilement which
keeps mankind from rising to the divine ideal.
Self-training in prayer, for anyone who wants to
become an expert, involves long and earnest
practice in this realisation of the oneness of
human sin as of the oneness of human character.
To feel all sin as my own, to feel myself a point
at which human sin reveals itself, is at the
opposite pole to the self-congratulation which
says ' I thank Thee that I am not as other men
are.' As far as the East is from the West so far
is true ' sympathy ' removed from pious horror.
But equally far is it removed from ' apathy,'
and from the weak amiability which condones
sin as a foible or a misfortune. To ' feel sin as
a lump ' is to feel it intensely as your own ; and
the more you can do so the nearer you will
reach to the infinite sympathy of the Lamb of
God, the sinless Penitent, who ' taketh away
the sin of the world ' by making it His own, and
destroying it by His life of obedience culminat-
ing on the Cross. That is what S. Paul meant
when He said that ' God made Him who knew
no sin to be sin on our behalf ' (2 Cor. v. 21).

Any crude notion of mere substitution is far removed from this wonderful aspect of the Atonement.

And what is true of all sin is true of all sorrow. Here we use the word 'sympathy' with the meaning that is more commonly attached to it. 'Surely He hath borne our griefs and carried our sorrows.' In His measureless love He not only knew, but *felt* Himself to be the Representative of mankind, and therefore felt the world's agony as His own. And every human being is necessarily a representative of mankind; but we seldom get beyond the point of knowing it theoretically. To make it real, and feel it, requires a life-long progress in love. And love grows by prayer, which brings us gradually to the realisation of the oneness of the life of men. As we keep these things and ponder them in our hearts we learn that self-training in prayer involves following our Lord to Calvary, and hanging with Him upon His Cross.

But this is what we mean by a 'priest. A priest is one who 'being taken from among men is appointed for men in things pertaining to God' (Heb. v. 1). And from among the whole body of mankind a particular group of people has been divinely appointed to be ' a kingdom

of priests,' that is the Christian Church, which
in turn chooses and appoints its representatives
whom we call priests. The Church is the
priest of mankind. And every Christian—
man, woman and child—ought to be taught
that his whole and sole function, in things pertaining to God, is to exercise the priestly office.
Every Christian, in so far as he is truly Christian,
is a point at which mankind comes into union
with God. Through Christians the Self-expression of the personal God is deepened and in-
tensified as the ages go by, because the Church is
in living and progressive union with the perfect
expression of God, Jesus Christ the Priest.

Self-training in prayer, therefore, requires us
to ponder on our priesthood, and on the
' sympathy ' which it involves, and to give it a
living place in our understanding and life.

IX. PRAYER AND WORK.

IN the first five chapters our thoughts dwelt mainly upon God as the one infinite personal Reality. In the next three we considered Mankind as the instrument of His Self-expression. All this has shown us that prayer is a very big thing, a life-long profession needing the most patient and strenuous self-training. The way is now clear to think of prayer as ordinarily understood, that is the various methods of prayer. But as a preliminary the relation between prayer and work calls for attention.

This is a matter of importance at any time, but the war has raised it to a problem of the first rank. Everyone is busy, or nearly everyone. The war looms like a storm-cloud, electric and depressing; and from across the water we can almost hear the fearful mutterings of thunder. And those at home feel as a heavy weight the necessity of doing something, to help either those who are fighting or those who come back sick and broken from the fight. And some people are tempted to think : ' Prayer ? Oh yes, very important of course ; but just now I absolutely haven't the time ! ' And they are inclined to add, ' After all when one is working for others it is a relief to think that *laborare est orare,* to work is to pray.' Now when a person thinks that he is too busy to pray, he feels it annoying to be referred to the story of Martha and Mary, and cannot help sympathizing very much with Martha. But I am sure that that story is constantly misused. Are we really to suppose that Mary spent the whole of her life sitting still and doing nothing but contemplate, or read her Bible, while Martha spent the whole of her life in house-work ? Her grumble against Mary, ' Lord, carest Thou not that my sister hath left me to serve alone ? ' shows that she was not accustomed to be left to serve alone, and that Mary usually helped her. Martha and Mary must not be taken as types of two people, the one all work and the other all prayer. They are a photograph, a snap-shot, so to speak, of two states of mind at a particular moment— the moment when the chance offered itself of a quiet, satisfying conversation with our Lord. Mary seized it and Martha didn't. They represent, in fact, two different attitudes to-wards the divine Reality. A few people have received a vocation to spend their lives in prayer, and nothing but prayer. But the majority, whose vocation is to what is called an active life of work, can themselves be likened to either Martha or Mary according as their work is lacking in prayer or filled with prayer. The question is What is the meaning of work filled with prayer? Now I cannot speak smooth things; I must put before you the highest Christian ideal. It means work done in such a condition of soul that in every detail, in every hour and moment and second, you are filled with the Presence of God, you are in touch with the divine Reality. To make quite true in your life the saying that To work is to pray, is to be Martha and Mary at the same time; and that is the climax of Christian perfection. It gives a new meaning to the Gospels to read the accounts of our Lord's busy life, remembering that that was literally true of Him; never for an instant was He out of touch with God. But how did He do it? Even He did not spend His whole life in work. Because He was human, because He was tempted like as we are, and hemmed in by physical limitations as we are, He spent long, long hours of silent solitude and prayer, keeping Himself in unvarying union with the divine Reality. And if He needed it, how can we dare to spend a busy day without it ? We must follow Mary every day, if we are to do Martha's work without the Lord's rebuke. If in all the busy racket of work we are to dwell under the defence of the Most High, and abide under the shadow of the Almighty, we must retain that defence, and hide ourselves under that shadow, by *making time* for deep, quiet prayer. It is the stern practice in private that makes the world-famed professional. And if it is our profession to ' follow the example of our Saviour Christ and to be made like unto Him,' in other words to be priests always in touch with God on behalf of mankind, an absolute necessity in our self-training is practice in private.

X. METHODS OF PRAYER.

IT is this practice of prayer in its various methods that we are now to study. Different writers have classified prayer in different ways. But perhaps the most helpful classification is one which may be connected with our Lord's words, 'Ask and it shall be given you, seek and ye shall find, knock and it shall be opened unto you.' We may call the three classes Prayer of utterance, Prayer of thought, and Prayer of union.

Prayer of utterance comprises all prayer that takes the form of words, whether actually vocal and audible, or uttered internally in the mind. This includes petitions for oneself, intercession for others, and praise and thanksgiving to God. And I think that for large numbers of Christians who have not made much effort at self-training this virtually exhausts the whole of prayer. And even in this class, the practice of one or two or all three of them divides Christians into three grades. The least trained do not rise beyond petitions for their personal needs, and that mostly when the needs are sudden and pressing. That is the sort of prayer that a good many of the soldiers in the trenches are learning for the first time, as several of them have told me. That their prayers are often intensely earnest, and that God hears them, no Christian would think of doubting. But if, when they come home, their prayers do not advance beyond that, all the peril and strain will not have carried them very far in their spiritual progress. But anyone who can add to his prayer intercession for others, has taken a great step forward. And the intercessions increase in width and range with the Christian's spiritual growth. But thirdly, to add praise and thanksgiving to God with any reality of meaning marks a much further advance.

XI. EARNESTNESS.

NOW, what is it that makes prayer effectual? Or, in other words, what sort of prayer accomplishes most?

It is easy to give a wrong answer to the question, and to think that effectiveness in prayer depends simply on the earnestness with which we pray. But take an instance. A mother is in an agony of mind because her little child falls dangerously ill; and she prays for his recovery with an earnestness equal to her agony of mind. And she may be inclined to feel, Surely, surely, God can't refuse me what I long for so intensely! Just down the street there is a workhouse, where a little child is dangerously ill in the infirmary. His parents are dead, and no one in the world is fond of him enough to pour out passionate, agonized, petitions for him. Do you suppose that God is going to restore the first child to health, but let the second die because any prayers that may have been offered for him were not earnest enough? When it comes to earnestness, petitions for ourselves and intercessions for others are sometimes hardly distinguishable. It is natural and human to feel a desire most acutely when it is for something which bears upon one-self. And this is, for the most part, true even in the matter of praise and thanksgiving to God. We are generally moved to thank Him most warmly for blessings which affect us individually. If the former of the two children recovers, we can picture the eager joy with which the mother will pour out her thanks, whereas no one, perhaps, will feel the same joy over the motherless waif. We do not, of course, find fault with the earnestness of personal desire ; but we must not think of it as capable *in itself* of persuading God to give us what He might not have given us otherwise.

Further, if earnestness of personal desire is the one thing needful, what are we to think of the effects produced by our public worship ? I am very far from saying that our prayers, private and public, are not in need of more earnestness ; but it must be an earnestness of the right kind ; one that is not excited by the faintest touch of Self. In our training and practice in prayer few things are harder, and few things are more important, than this escape from Self. Our earnestness must be the earnestness not of individuals but of priests.

XII. THE TRUE MOTIVE.

AND so we go back to the subject of chapters
vi.-viii., Mankind, as one real whole,
growing up towards the perfect Man. The
nearer we can get to a passionate earnestness
for that, the more will our prayer accomplish.
Look at S. Paul. He wrote to the Colossians
(ii. 1), ' I want you to know how great a con-
flict I have—*i.e.* with what agony of earnestness I pray—for you, and them at Laodicea,
and as many as have not seen my face in the
flesh.' He had not founded either of those
Churches, and his earnestness, therefore, was
not caused by the fact that he was praying for
personal friends, but was due to his burning
desire for the building up of the whole Body of
Christ, through which all mankind could be
lifted into union with God. Think of your
prayers for foreign missions, and for the
Church's work at home, your prayers for the
wounded and the prisoners, for the soldiers,
doctors, nurses, chaplains, at home and at the
front. Test your state of advance with regard

to self-training in prayer. Is the lifting up of mankind as one whole into union with God a motive real and pressing enough to give you a deep earnestness in these intercessions? And your prayers for victory. What is their motive? They may spring from various degrees of selfishness. But the only sort of prayer that will accomplish anything is that the result of the war, whether victory or defeat, and if the former the nature of the victory and its immediate consequences, may be guided by God to serve the purposes of His kingdom, the lifting up of all mankind into union with Him.

And your prayers for the departed. It ought not to have needed the war to bring back this practice into English Christian life. If mankind is one, it is not only the little group of human lives at present on the planet in flesh and blood, but all souls past and present, who must be lifted up into union with God. Our prayers for them and theirs for us are alike intercessions for mankind as one whole.

Further, if this and nothing less than this is really our longing desire, we shall free ourselves from what is for some earnest Christians a great difficulty and snare. We shall be able to avoid the distracted feeling that, owing to the multitude of things and persons that need our prayers, we cannot, so to speak, cover the ground. It is right, of course, to offer particular intercessions on matters which come under our individual notice, and are commended to our sympathy, provided we place them in their true relation to the Whole. But we must not let ourselves wander into discursiveness, which too often means perfunctoriness ; we must throw off the burden of mere multiplicity. That is a form of the ' much speaking ' in prayer which our Lord condemns. Our intercessions are not valuable in proportion to the number of things that we pray about.

XIII. PUBLIC WORSHIP.

THAT is where public worship ought to be a help rather than a difficulty. In public worship we join, as members of the Church, in a corporate act, ' to make prayers and supplications and to give thanks for all men ' as our Prayer Book puts it. Try hard to make more real the conception of the Church as the priest of humanity ; try hard to feel that the Church is not a collection of pious individuals, but a single organism working for the spiritual advance of the whole body of mankind ; and Church services, even the sober intellectual restraint of Morning and Evening Prayer and the Litany, will become a new thing to you.

Above all, the Holy Communion must be freed from every vestige of Self. It is in its essence a corporate act in behalf of all men, one aspect of which is intercession. Whatever your particular shade of views about the doctrine of the Holy Sacrament, to leave it out of your life, or to throw it in occasionally as an extra, is to neglect the most non-selfish act of intercession that you can make. Throughout the length and breadth of our religion the spiritual and the sacramental are complementary to each other. The Christian, therefore, who practises intercession without sacramental intercession cannot, from the nature of the case, reach the fullest success in his self-training.

Again, if any advance in prayer must begin, for each of us, with penitence and self-mortification, the same is true of corporate prayer. It ought to be the result of true sympathy, the feeling of the shame of the world's sin, of which we thought in chapter viii. The avoidance of a corporate act of penitence by English Christians, lest the enemy should think we were down-hearted, or doubted the rightness of our national cause, was a mournful exhibition of ignorance as to the nature of prayer.

Probably most Christians would admit that one of their greatest needs in the spiritual life is the self-training which will enable them to make public worship what it is intended to be. We must immerse ourselves, gradually, by practice, in the reality of the corporate life of the Church acting for mankind as one Whole in things pertaining to God. In chapter ii we thought of the concentration by which it is possible to gaze with the eye of the soul through Nature to the divine Reality. And the same is true with regard to Mankind. It would be a great help in practice if some members of a congregation would agree beforehand to come to an ordinary Church service with the united intention of concentrating themselves upon mankind as a whole, striving to make every petition bear upon that. They would find our Lord's words come home to them with wonderful force, ' If two of you shall agree upon earth concerning any matter that they shall ask, it shall be done for them by My Father which is in heaven.' The concentration of two is more than double the concentration of one ; they can help each other to reach out to the divine Reality.

But this is a matter which needs long and patient practice. If the reader to whom this point of view is new will study his Prayer Book, as though for the first time, in such a way as to learn to make ' We,' ' Us,' and ' Our ' refer in every case not to the individual worshippers gathered at the moment in church, much less to himself alone, but to Mankind of which we are members, and to make every petition in which the personal pronoun does not occur definitely contribute to the working out of God's plan of lifting up the whole of Mankind, he will realise how large and noble an element of public worship has hitherto been lost to him.

XIV. THY WILL BE DONE.

THE same motive will safeguard our private petitions for ourselves. They will not be individual but personal, that is, they will be petitions that something may be granted to us which will somehow, in the manifold wisdom of God, advance the one personal life of mankind. That is really the meaning of saying ' Grant me this if it is Thy will,' and also ' Grant me this for Jesus Christ's sake.' God's will is always that ' all men should be saved,' all men as one whole should grow towards the perfect Man ; and nothing which will not contribute to that will receive the endorsement of the perfect Man, and be included in the intercessions which, with unutterable groanings, the Holy Spirit offers for and in us ; and hence nothing which will not contribute to that will be granted to us as an answer to prayer. This motive will give us perfect peace and submission in the numberless cases in which we do not get just what we ask for. 'Ask and it shall be given you' means Ask with God's will for mankind in view, and ye shall receive, not necessarily your exact request, but that which you really want far more—something that will help to work out His will.

But it is impossible that that motive can really move us unless we are in close contact with Him—not holding the right views about Him, not a general benevolence which can extend itself widely over mankind, but real, inner, living contact with Him ; in other words, real, inner, living love for Him, a love which wants nothing but that His will may be done, and wants that with all the strength of our being, and a love which is always ready to praise and thank Him for every exhibition of His will, whether it sends to us what we commonly call blessings, or whether, for His own loving purposes, it places us, and all the nations of the earth, with Him on the Cross.

XV. PRAYER OF THOUGHT.

'ASK and it shall be given you, seek and ye shall find.' The first has suggested Prayer of utterance, or verbal prayer. The second suggests what I have called Prayer of thought.

The search for truth has been the occupation of all thinking people in all countries at all times. In every branch of learning students profess, as the object of their lives, to be seekers after truth ; some call themselves seekers after God. But in every branch of learning intellectual search will teach men only facts about God and His actions, it will not find God Himself. We saw how true this is in thinking about a rose. Biologist, botanist, mathematician, chemist, or all combined, cannot make you know what a rose really is. And if this is the case with the divine Reality in Nature it is not less so with the divine personal Reality in man. To reach that, requires our will and our emotions more than our intellect ; it requires something which is of the nature of spiritual thought rather than of study. And this is afforded by what is usually called Meditation, in which the intellectual faculty is not excluded but takes the lowest place.

Large numbers of Christians think of meditation as an elaborate and artificial exercise of pious ingenuity for which a few religiously-minded people seem to have time and inclination, but which for most people is quite out of the question. I will not pretend that it is easy. The easy things are not always the most worth doing. But whatever else may be said about it, 'elaborate' and 'artificial' are the last epithets that it deserves. Utter simplicity is the first mark of true meditation. The reason why it is not easy is that, being a method of reaching after contact with God, it requires all the preliminary conditions of penitence and humility. It requires a real longing to find the very God Himself, and it requires considerable determination, especially for beginners.

An illustration may help to show what it means. Americans have the reputation, when they travel, of flying from place to place, seeing the famous sights as fast as trains and motors will carry them. They want to have seen as many things as possible. But this continual hustling allows of no real, intimate, inner knowledge of any one thing or place. That is like a person who reads through some prayers, or a passage in the Bible, and feels that he has done his duty to God for the day. But has he? Has he found God? Has he gained afresh any real, intimate, inner knowledge of Him? To do that, he must constantly pause over a verse, a phrase, even a word, and gaze right into its meaning, and get something out of it for his soul. He must go so slowly that it becomes a means of seeking after Reality, and finding in scene after scene, or sentence after sentence, a message from God which he, in turn, can translate into fervent prayer for himself and for others, into an earnest longing, or a hope, or a resolve, or a cry of penitence. It does not need elaborate study, or cleverness; it does not need any careful arrangement of your thoughts such as you would want if you had to preach a sermon or give a lesson; indeed it is a misuse of meditation to make it a means of preparing a sermon or a lesson. But it needs an eager desire to use the words, through which you are very slowly wandering, as a medium by which to get yourself into closer contact with God. It doesn't matter what you do with the passage; your treatment of it is known only to God and yourself. It doesn't matter whether you can exercise much brilliant imagination or none at

all. The only thing you have to do is to make
the passage, or sentence, or word, by any means
you like, and by as many means as you can contrive, helpful to your spiritual life, that is to
your will and your love, your determination and
your longing to reach after God. You need not
expect to gain much pleasure from it at first ;
possibly you may never gain much pleasure from
it. The facility in meditation of the spontaneous
kind that makes it a daily delight to some people
is not given to everyone. But the patient
continuance in effort is itself a discipline of in-
calculable value. And even to those who find
the effort very hard indeed there comes from
time to time a flash of spiritual insight which
lights up a sentence, and makes the way easier.
For the purpose of meditation the New Testa-
ment, since it deals directly with Jesus Christ,
especially a Gospel, is more likely to be helpful
than anything else, because He is the perfect
revelation of God, and therefore it is easier to
reach God by pondering on Him than on any
other thing or person.

It is possible also to make use sometimes
of a devotional book and not the Bible. But
it is generally the best plan not to depend upon
other people's meditations, but to undergo the
effort of making your own, however imperfectly.

All the great saints in the Church's history, and all the holiest men and women alive to-day, have made use of meditation as an absolutely indispensable part of their self-training. And no Christian who really wants to train himself in prayer can do without it.

Some people find it wise not to make a rule to give to it a fixed time every day, because in a busy life there are days when this is almost impossible ; but make a rule, and often ask for the strength of God to help you to keep it, to spend on meditation a fixed time every week, so that you are free to vary the daily time when needful.

Modern Biblical study, which is now so widely spread, however useful in itself, tends to place a difficulty in the way. People are apt to get the notion that Bible reading always involves a study of the Synoptic problem, or Jewish Eschatology, or the geography of Asia Minor, or something else up-to-date and academic. Devotional Bible reading, let me repeat, involves literally nothing but a longing determination to get, through penitence, humility, and quiet thought, into closer touch with God.

XVI. PRAYER OF UNION.

WE turn now to the third clause in our Lord's sentence : ' Knock and it shall be opened unto you,' which suggests what I have called Prayer of union. Meditation requires the intellectual faculty—not to be excluded but—to be kept rather in the background as compared with the free play given to the will and the emotions in their reaching after God. But Prayer of union, or contemplation, is a further stage in which the intellectual faculty is not allowed to assert itself at all. ' Commune with your own heart and in your chamber, and be still.' That exhortation is not fully met either by petitions or meditations. There is something else, which it is exceedingly difficult to explain in words, and which can really be learnt by nothing but practice and experience, built upon the basis of true penitence and humility. If I were to ask a musician to explain what method I must adopt to gain a deep inner understanding of the meaning and glory of a symphony of Beethoven, he would not find it easy. But obviously he would begin his explanation by telling me that first of all I must *listen in silence*. And yet though that is obvious in the case of music, it is not at all obvious to many Christians in the case of spiritual contact with God.

This subject has often been written about. It is the burden of a large number of mediæval books on the spiritual life. It has been called Quietism, and other bad names. It is an important element in the religious practice of the Society of Friends. And it has recently been revived within the Church. But there is still room, perhaps, for a re-statement of it, if only to guard against mistakes. For there are some bad mistakes into which it is easy to fall.

It may be well to suggest a definition as a basis for study. Prayer of union, or of silence, or of contemplation—it has many names ; some writers have called it ' interior prayer '—is an attitude towards God in which intellectual thought and emotional feeling are kept in abeyance, the will is exercised in keeping them so, and the love of the whole being is free to unite itself with the love of God. The last may be expressed metaphorically by saying that love silently and persistently knocks at the door, that it may be opened for God's love to stream out.

XVII. MISTAKES.

AND first, what to avoid. Three mistakes are often made, especially by beginners, in attempting the practice of contemplation.

1. We saw that in meditation all artificiality must be avoided. And the same is even more urgently necessary here, for artificiality is so closely akin to self-consciousness; and nothing is more fatal to the free play of humble and penitent love. When a person first begins this kind of self-training, he is at once troubled with the feeling—'I am now doing something really advanced in the Christian life, something novel and exciting, something that most Christians don't even attempt.' But the moment the attempt becomes a pious pose, its value is instantly blotted out, and the door between the soul and the divine Reality is locked and double-locked by man himself, with no possibility of opening. Instead of doing something really advanced and novel, he is away back in the very old and very elementary condition of self-love, pride and foolishness, the condition, in fact, of the Pharisee in the temple.

2. But some who free themselves, by God's help, from self-love and pride, do not quite escape the foolishness. They fall into a mistake arising from their very anxiety to gain the blessing that they seek. They imagine that the results of contemplation must take a striking or unusual form, a wonder, a thrill, a sweetness ; and in their eagerness they strain after it with a mental, and even physical, tension. Some even adopt physical means to carry themselves away from their surroundings ; they gaze at a crucifix, or an altar, or its lights, or a stained window, or a picture. Of course any of these may suggest material for helpful meditation. But if they are used as a means of inducing a process which is difficult to distinguish from hypnotic self-suggestion, they have no more right to be considered as a legitimate method of Christian contemplation than crystal-gazing. I think it should be clear that this is artificiality appearing in another guise, and one which may do great injury to a nervous, highly strung temperament. It is just such a temperament which lends itself most readily to the mistake. One of the commonest objections to religion is that it is merely a matter of temperament ; and mistaken enthusiasm of this kind, which is as strictly artificial as alcoholic

excitement, gives a serious handle to the charge. As S. Teresa said, ' From silly devotions God deliver us ! ' And in the same spirit of commonsense Ruysbroek advises learners to adopt for contemplation any physical posture that will best make for quiet of mind and body, that neither mind nor body may intrude itself and interrupt the interior communing. He recognises that some people can contemplate best when walking about, or standing, or kneeling ; but he himself found it easier, and therefore simpler and more helpful, to sit. Anything will do, provided that it helps to reduce the physical element in contemplation to a minimum.

3. A third mistake, closely allied to the last, is to expect, or even to want or hope for, visions, trances, ecstasies or the like. These were related of many of the mediæval saints, as also of Christians in earlier days ; and they are by no means unknown in modern times. But those who have written about contemplation, and recorded their experiences, are unanimous in declaring that such experiences are never to be sought for, and cannot be gained by trying. I will not attempt to discuss the psychology of them. That branch of study is still far too young to afford safe ground for any definite

decision as to how far they are pathological, the results of temperament or of something in the nature of self-suggestion, and whether, or to what extent, they are an immediate divine gift. I want only to make clear that in either case they lie entirely outside the limits of our self-training.

IF we are right, then, in assuming that these three things—self-satisfaction, self-excitement, and the seeking for abnormal experiences —are bad mistakes to be resolutely avoided, what can be said as to the true nature of contemplation or Prayer of union ? It has two aspects, which are strictly and literally mutual, and inconceivable each without the other.

1. Recall what was said in chapter vi about Influence, the influx, the flowing in, of personality into personality, the interpenetration of souls. Now, when someone exercises a strong influence over me, I may recognise the fact if I think about it, I may realise that when I speak or act or think in a particular way it is because he has influenced me. Again, I may, by a conscious act of will, put myself, or allow myself to be drawn, under his influence. And once more, I may experience a feeling of pleasure in doing so. But what is it in me which has actually received his influence ? It is not my thinking consciousness, nor my will, nor my feelings, but my whole Self, my Ego, to its deepest depths and its fullest content,

not differentiated into its several aspects. This need not be described as my sub-consciousness, or subliminal or supraliminal consciousness, because we do not know enough about it to give it any such spatial name. It is better to call it simply my Ego, or my spirit.

And the reception of God's influence, or in other words the influx of His Spirit, is analogous to this reception of human influence. One of the two aspects of contemplation is that in silence, with no striving of thought or will or feeling for the purpose of obtaining an effect, but with a concentration of the whole being, *not on a purpose but on a Person*, you receive His Spirit into your spirit ; your spirit lies open and susceptible to the influence of His Spirit. When you afterwards think about it, you know that it has been so by its effects upon you ; you can then feel and enjoy the tremendous fact of His Presence growing, deepening, brightening —how can language describe it ?—as the years go by. And you find also that when you turn to the other methods of prayer that we have thought of, petition, intercession, praise, thanksgiving, meditation, you come to them enveloped in an atmosphere of God's Presence which gives to all of them an increasing reality. But *the very act itself*, the reception of God's influence, is the reception of what is divine, and what on that account your human thinking consciousness cannot possibly grasp.

It is a matter of perfect peace; no excitement, or straining, or striving, or contriving; and on the other hand no lazy dreaminess or hypnotic lethargy. Contemplation can often be reached by passing straight on from meditation. Some of the greatest writers on the subject have earnestly advised that as the best way of escaping the danger of mere dreaminess. You pause so long over a sentence or a thought suggested by what you are reading that the earthly language begins to fade as the brightness of His Presence grows. Meditation brings you into contact with Reality, and contemplation keeps you there. It is letting your soul stand in an attitude to receive God. It is knocking at the door, and waiting for God to open.

2. The second aspect of contemplation is inseparable from the first. Take the words in our Communion Office, 'Here we offer and present unto Thee, O Lord, ourselves.' Our mind can think about doing this, our will can determine to do it; our feelings can enjoy the thought, and the determination. But *the very act itself*, the very offering and presenting,

which takes place in silent contemplation, is the work of the Ego, the spirit, the whole Self, not differentiated into its several aspects, giving itself to God's Spirit. The Lord says, ' Behold I stand at the door and knock.' In contemplation we realise that He on His part is waiting for us to open ; and we hear Him say ' Is thy heart right, as My heart is with thy heart ? '

But what is this mutuality of receiving and offering, the method of which I have called Prayer of union ? There is only one word for it—Love. The method is not dreamy laziness, or anything quietistic or hypnotic ; it is the give-and-take of Love. As S. Bernard puts it, it is ' God loving Himself [by a love proceeding] from man.'

XIX. FELLOWSHIP.

IF it is truly this, it is not selfish, because all mankind is one, the instrument of the Self-expression of the personal Reality. The principle of representation, of ' sympathy,' of priesthood, comes into play here as in all other methods of prayer. Our Prayer of union works towards the closer union of God with all mankind.

Some members of the Church have recently made the attempt to realise the true corporateness of prayer, by meeting together for the purpose, and joining in what has been called the Fellowship of Silence. It would be of untold value if the silence could sometimes be made an opportunity for united contemplation. There is no reason, in the nature of things, why the practice of public worship should not be extended to include all the three methods of prayer. A group of people unite in knocking at the door, and opening to God's knock. And if they really contemplate, really meet with God in the give-and-take of Love, they are at the same time mutually pouring their influence into each other, and therefore drawing each other nearer to God. One word of warning is needed. When they first begin to try, and probably for some time, they will find the difficulty of escaping self-consciousness much greater than in solitude. But if they can overcome that by practice and habit, their souls will rise in unison to God.

Lastly, let it never be forgotten that, as in the case of intercession, spiritual communion has its necessary complement in sacramental communion, wherein, as a united whole, we offer ourselves to God in union with Christ's eternal Self-offering, and as a united whole receive His Life. It is the sacrament of the give-and-take of Love.

The Christian Church must continue to train itself in prayer, thereby drawing all men into the vortex of the Love of God, ' till we all come in the unity of the Faith and of the knowledge of the Son of God, unto a perfect Man, unto the measure of the stature of the fulness of Christ.'

"Thou must understand that in meditation no certain rule can be set for everyone to observe, for they are in the free gift of our Lord, according to divers dispositions of chosen souls, and according as we thrive in that state and in virtues, so God increaseth our meditations, both in spiritual knowing and loving Him."

"The third sort of prayer is only in the heart without speech, with great rest and quietness both of soul and body. A pure heart it behoveth him to have that shall pray after this manner."

HILTON.

"And whoso will be a perfect disciple of our Lord's, him behoveth strain up his spirit in this work ghostly, for the salvation of all his brethren and sisters in nature, as our Lord did His body on the Cross. And how? Not only for His friends and His kin and His homely lovers, but generally for all mankind, without any special beholding more to one than to another."

"The whiles our desire is mingled with any matter of bodilyness, as it is when we stress and strain us in spirit and in body together, so long is it farther from God than it should be an it were done more devoutly and more listily in soberness and in purity and in deepness of spirit."

THE CLOUD OF UNKNOWING.

"Our Lord Himself He is the first receiver of our prayer, as to my sight, and He taketh it full thankfully; and highly enjoying, He sendeth it up above, and setteth it in treasure, where it shall never perish."

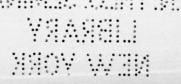

"Thus the soul by prayer is accorded with God. But when our courteous Lord of His special grace sheweth Himself to our soul, we have that we desire; and then we see not for the time what we should more pray; but all our intent, with all our mights, is set whole into the beholding of Him."

JULIANA OF NORWICH.

"I do not, and I cannot, understand how humility can exist without love, or love without humility."

S. TERESA.

"The Spirit comes in contact with our spirit and says to it in the depth: Love Me as I love thee,—as I have loved thee eternally. Now this voice, this prayer, this interior demand, is so terrible to hear that our spirit is utterly overthrown by the tempest of love; and all the powers of the soul, shaken and trembling, turn to each other, asking, Do we indeed love the eternal Love, the Love inexhaustible?"

"When love has allowed itself to be rapt above its created substance by transcendent joy, it finds and tastes upon the mountain the splendour and delights which God causes to flow into the inner sanctuaries of life, impressing upon the ravished soul a certain image of His own Majesty."

RUYSBROEK.

"As sure as it is our duty to look wholly unto God in our prayers, so sure is it that it is our duty to live wholly unto God in our lives."

LAW.

Printed by

W. Heffer and Sons Ltd.

104 Hills Road,

Cambridge.